DAX'S BIG ADVENTURE!

Written by Danielle Blattner
Illustrated by Jupiters Muse

Tellwell Talent
www.tellwell.ca

ISBN
978-0-2288-6409-7 (Hardcover)
978-0-2288-6408-0 (Paperback)

Hallie Fry | Hallie Fry Photography, Kansas City, MO

Preface:

Hey there! I'm Danielle, a brand-new mom to our son, Dax. We're a simple family living in Overland Park, Kansas. Although my husband [Tyson] and I were ready to start a family and planned for a baby, we were unprepared for the news we received when Dax was born. Dax was diagnosed with a very rare chromosomal disorder: Pontocerebellar Hypoplasia Type 8. There are only six previously recorded cases of this incurable genetic disease in medical literature. Doctors have asked us to remain cautiously optimistic as his time with us on Earth is very limited. Even though the news hit us like a freight train in room 35 of the NICU, Dax has been our biggest blessing. His diagnosis really put things into perspective for us.

Prior to staying home with Dax, I was a dental hygienist. I was accustomed to filling up our calendar at least six months in advance. I love structure, making plans, and crossing things off of a to-do list. As a first-time mom, I did all of the research. I had the bottles and pacifiers washed, sterilized, and ready to go. Little did we know, all of those things would sit untouched. Dax is unable to swallow; he has a G-tube. We use an enteral feeding pump to feed him. We quickly realized that life is full of the unexpected, and I learned things don't always go as planned. Six months from now, there's nothing on the books for us. We choose to look at the calendar one day at a time.

The fourth trimester wasn't exactly pure bliss; it was a mixture of emotions for me. During the first few weeks of having Dax at home, it was difficult for me to connect with him. I didn't feel that special bond between us; it was like I put a wall up, trying to protect myself from the pain and heartache I knew I'd have to face one day. As I held my newborn baby in my arms, I grieved. I grieved Dax's diagnosis and the future I had pictured for our family. I was adjusting to life as a new mom and trying to wrap my head around what our new normal would look like, not only as parents but as caregivers. It took me quite some time to fully process and accept it all. I often wondered if I'd ever get through a day without crying. But, as the weeks continued, the worries didn't consume every thought and conversation I had. Pontocerebellar Hypoplasia suddenly didn't sound so foreign to me anymore. The odds of having a baby with this diagnosis are less than one in a million—we were meant to have Dax. We made a promise to each other and Dax that we'd always find silver linings in each day and stay positive; we're embracing each day that we have with him. Dax knows that he still brings joy and happiness to our lives despite his heartbreaking diagnosis. He's sweet, he's happy, and he loves to cuddle… he's perfect. And the bond I feared we wouldn't have is there and very strong. I feel most at peace with my son in my arms. Being "Mom" is the greatest title I've ever been given.

Our little boy has taught me more about life than I've learned in all of the 29 years that I've lived. Life is simple, life is sweet, and the littlest things can be joyful if you choose to be in the moment—to soak it in and appreciate it. We somehow learn to live in the future and to think ahead, but what about today? What's happening today that brings you joy and a sense of contentment? When's the last time you slowed down to simply bob your head around to one of your favorite songs? When's the last time you took a moment to sit outside to feel the warm sunshine on your skin and the blades of grass under your feet?

With all of the curveballs thrown our way, we decided not to waste any time. We purchased an RV, and my mother-in-law quickly coined it: The Dax-Mobile! We outlined our trip, **Dax's Big Adventure!**, and a few days later, we hit the road to show Dax the beauty our world has to offer.

Dedication:

Tyson, I simply couldn't do life without you. You're everything to me. The long days you put in don't go unnoticed. You give 110% and more every single day; you wake up hours before work to help with Dax so I can sleep, work all day, and then stay up late just to talk with me. You watch me cry, and you wipe my tears. You keep me grounded through all of the waves of emotions. You always know what to say to help my mind find peace; you're my anchor. You are the most incredible father to Dax; he loves you so much. I am eternally grateful that this experience with Dax has only brought us closer, has made our marriage stronger, and has strengthened our faith. I love you with all of my heart.

Dax, I promise you, sweet baby, your light will forever shine. You've opened up our eyes to what life is all about. The values we've learned from you on this journey will always be at the forefront of our family. You are a true miracle and our biggest blessing. Mommy and Daddy are by your side every step of the way. We love you beyond words. We are so proud of you, and I am *SO* proud to be your mom.

My Sincere Appreciation:

To our families, thank you for always being there for us, no matter what time of day. To our closest friends, thank you for staying in the picture and helping us carry on a bit of normalcy. Knowing we have such a strong support system to lean on brings us a significant amount of comfort.

To the sea of people who have reached out, thank you. To all of you who have come forward with your own struggles and your own stories, thank you for sharing. We've learned along the way that there are still so many genuine people in this world. Hearing your stories and realizing we aren't alone just confirms that you never know what someone else may be going through. Maybe the question "How are you?" should be rephrased to "I hope you're having a good day!".

 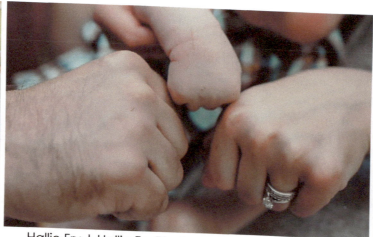 

Hallie Fry | Hallie Fry Photography, Kansas City, MO

Faith is giving us the strength to stand and put one foot in front of the other every single day. We're choosing to put our trust in Him as His plan unfolds.

The Dax-Mobile is all packed! Are you ready for your big adventure, Dax? It's time for you to see the beauty our world has to offer. We want to show you as much as we can! Grab the map of our route, Dax's feeding pump, and Ozzie's road-trip snacks. Let's get on the road!

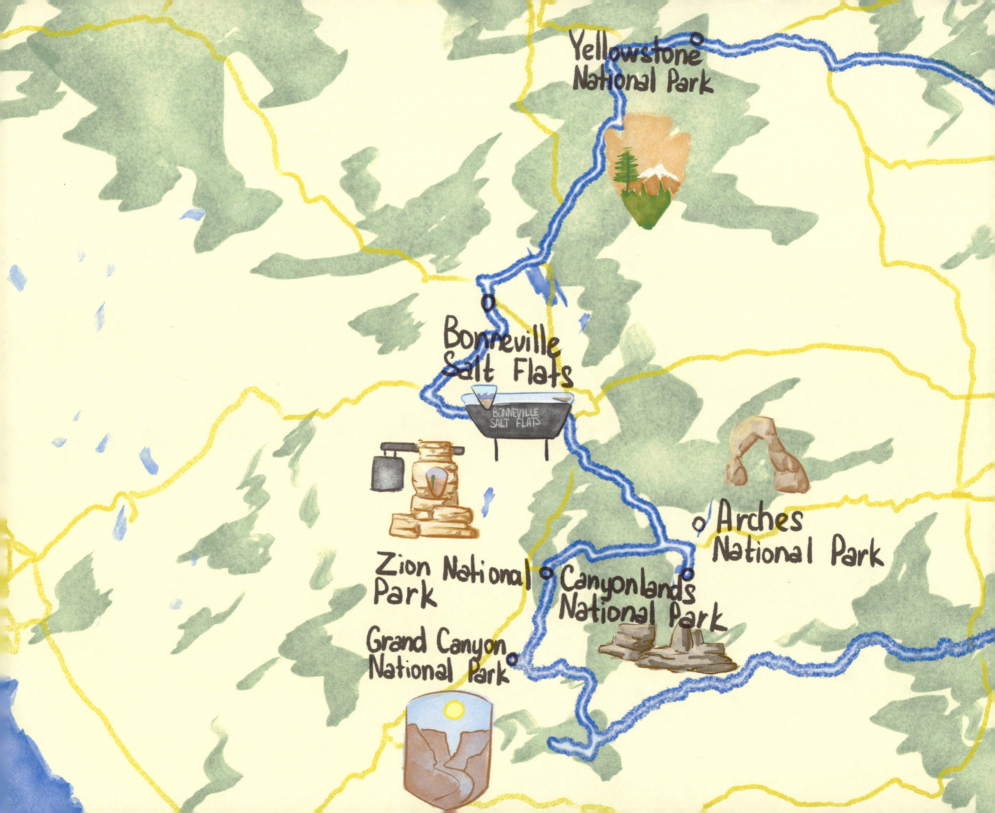

My goodness, what a long drive. I'm glad we're *finally* here. Dax, are you excited to see the Grand Canyon? We only have to walk about a mile and a half to get there.

Ozzie, I can hear those big paws shuffling on the pathway. We can't slow down yet, buddy! Our adventure is just getting started. Try to put a little pep in your step!

If we want to get to the lookout point before dark, you have no choice but to sit in the stroller with Dax. We have to keep up our pace!

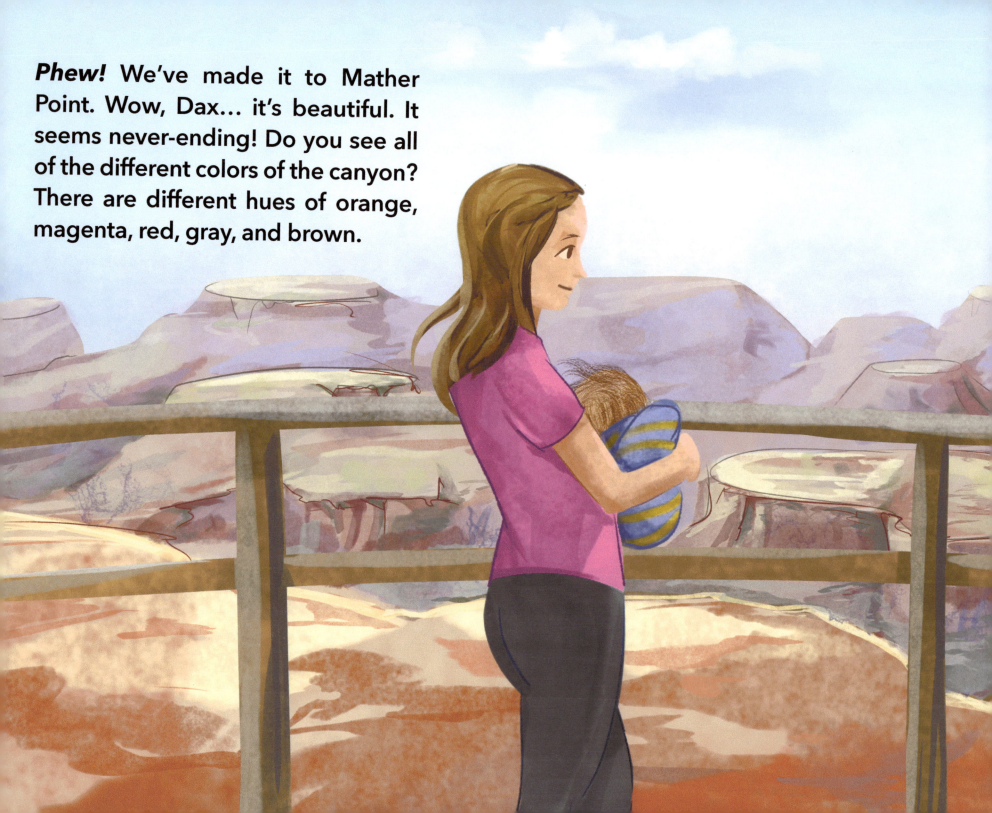

Phew! We've made it to Mather Point. Wow, Dax... it's beautiful. It seems never-ending! Do you see all of the different colors of the canyon? There are different hues of orange, magenta, red, gray, and brown.

Aah… the cool breeze feels so refreshing after our trek. Dax, your little brown locks are blowing in the wind!

Shhh, Ozzie. You're causing a scene with your loud huffing and puffing! I know you're excited, buddy; this is your first big adventure too! We aren't in Kansas anymore!

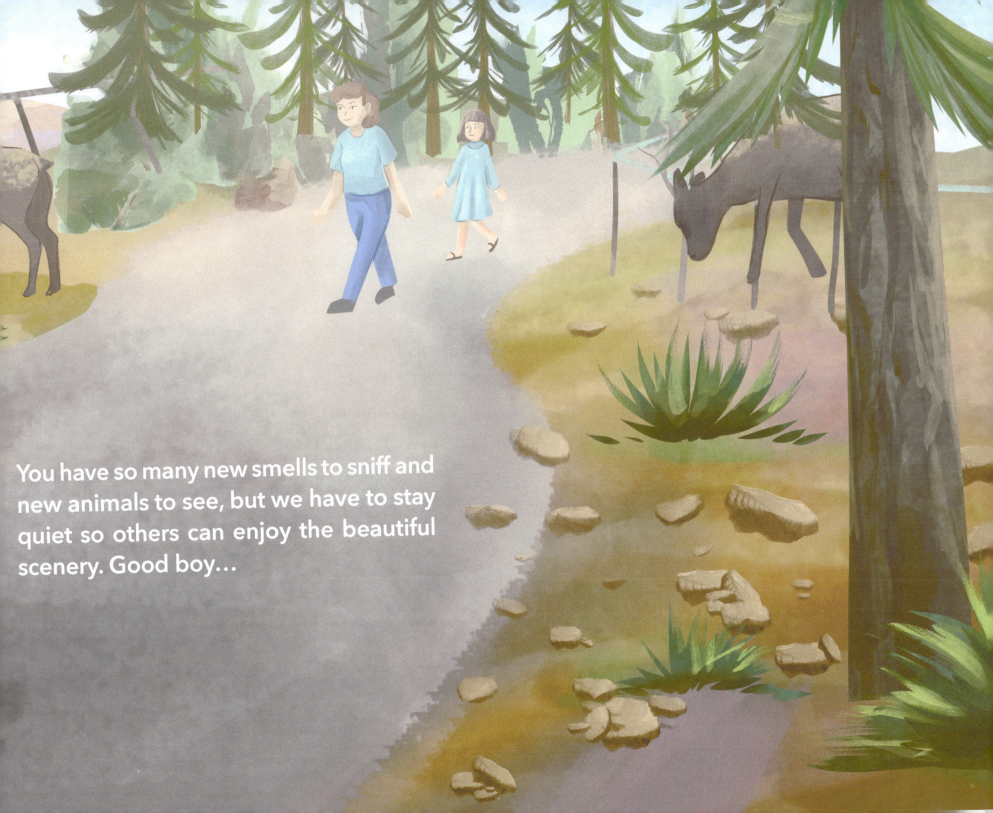

You have so many new smells to sniff and new animals to see, but we have to stay quiet so others can enjoy the beautiful scenery. Good boy…

Oh look, Dax! There's a rock you can touch. You've never felt anything like that before; give me your hand! **Oooo**... do you feel the rugged texture of Mother Nature?

Come on, Ozzie! Back in the stroller you go! We have to get back to the Dax-Mobile before the sun goes down. We're driving to Utah in the morning.

We're here, Dax! It feels like it's 100 degrees outside. Let's stay in the Dax-Mobile until it cools off some.

It's 4:55 pm, and it's starting to cool off. Let's check out the campground!

Dax, look all around. Do you see those wild rock formations? They look like big orange mountains. There are different tones and layers of orange, red, and tan. Do you see the contrast in all of the colors? You have the best view from way up there!

There's an ice cream shop across the street; that'll be the perfect treat to fuel us for the trails later. You can get a sundae too, Ozzie! I know your eyes tend to gaze at all the tourists, buddy, but don't forget to look at the spectacular landscape!

Wow, Ozzie! You ate your ice cream in record time! Come here, big boy! There's ice cream all over your face. I'll get you cleaned up before we walk back to the Dax-Mobile; we need to get some rest before exploring Zion.

Take a little snooze, Dax. Then we'll sightsee!

Zzzz-Zzzz-Zzzz

Zzzz-Zzzz-Zzzz

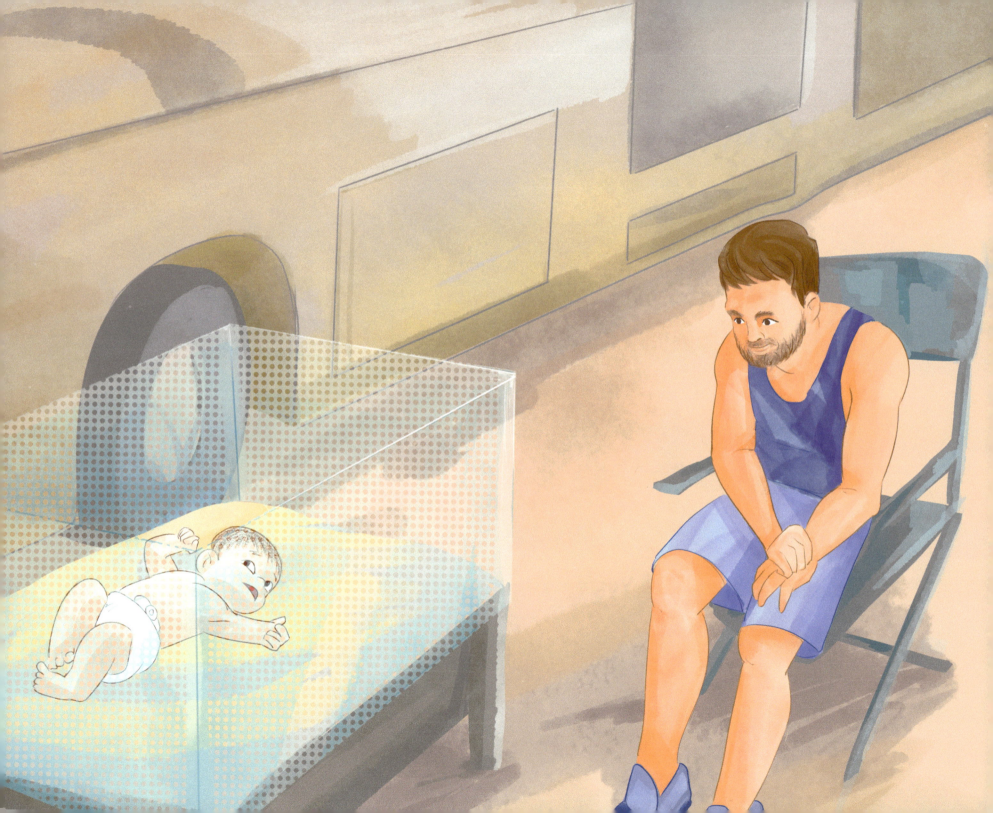

Dax is up from his nap! Let's go to Pa'rus Trail. It's the only pet-friendly trail in Zion National Park.

Dax, you're at Zion National Park!

Pa'rus
⇐ Trail

It looks like Ozzie's riding in the stroller with you—he's exhausted already!

We didn't walk very far to get here, Ozzie. I thought the sundae would give you enough energy for the trail, too. Sit back, relax, and enjoy your ride with Dax.

Fill up the fuel tank, Tyson! I have the turn-by-turn directions to get us across the state. Put the Dax-Mobile in drive!

We have officially arrived at the next stop on our adventure—Moab, Utah.

Ozzie, your dad upgraded your seat in the stroller to the back seat of a Jeep. He rented a Jeep Wrangler! This is really turning into an adventure, Dax; we can go off-roading! Wanna go on a car ride, Ozzie?! Okay, stop jumping around so your dad can pick you up!

Shafer Trail in Canyonlands National Park isn't far from our campsite; we'll go off-roading there. Is there plenty of gas in the tank? The trail is 19 miles long; we'll have to weave our way up 1,500 feet to get to the top!

Tyson, I can't look! This dirt road is so narrow! Where are the guard rails?! Slow down!

Dax seems to be unfazed by my fear; he's still smiling. I think he likes feeling the Jeep bounce around; he looks so happy! Dax must love the thrill of a good escapade, like you, Tyson. I'm just ready to get out of here!

Hallelujah! We made it! After two and a half hours on the rough terrain, I thought we'd never make it out of there! The views were amazing, but that was definitely a once-in-a-lifetime experience. We're *never* driving on the Shafer switchbacks again!

Arches National Park is only about 30 minutes away. We'll go there next! But first, let's drop Ozzie off at the Dax-Mobile; he can barely keep his eyes open.

Tyson, did you know that there are over 2,000 stone arches here? Mother Nature is incredible!

There's Delicate Arch, Dax! It's 52 feet tall, isn't it magnificent? Before we leave the park, you have to see Balanced Rock too!

Tyson, pose in front of Balanced Rock with Dax; hold him up like he's sitting on top, and I'll take your picture. It'll be *so* cute!

Perfect! Great job, you two! It's time to get back to the Dax-Mobile and see what Ozzie's up to. We have a big day tomorrow, we're driving to the Bonneville Salt Flats.

Holy cow! There's salt for miles! Beautiful, bright white, sparkly granules of salt, as far as the eye can see. Dax, can you feel the warm sunshine reflecting off the salt flats? Look at the mountains surrounding us. Mother Nature is magical!

Goodness gracious, Ozzie, you're so dramatic. I know you're not used to walking around in baby socks, but we don't want your paws to get burned from walking on the salt. Trust me, even though you can barely take one step forward, the socks *are* helping you.

On the road again!

Oh no, it's snowing, and it's piling up fast! It looks like the road is closed. We were **so** close to the campground, only 12 miles away! We just had hot summer weather in Utah, and now we're driving in a snowstorm in Montana that's making national news?! A foot of snow in May?! Unbelievable! Dax, you're experiencing all kinds of weather! We'll see where the alternate route takes us…

Woo-hoo! We're finally here! I can't believe it took us 4 hours to follow an 80-mile detour in this blizzard. I'm so grateful we made it here safely.

It's way past our bedtime; it's midnight already! Time to hit the hay! Sweet dreams, Dax.

Rise and shine! Mother Nature is cooperating; it's 61 degrees outside! Good thing the snow is melting because we didn't pack any snow gear!

Your dad rented another car. We'll get you two in the SUV and drive through Yellowstone.

Dax, look at the lush green hills filled with pine trees. And look over there! Do you see the snow-capped mountains? Look closer; there's a herd of bison!

Park the car here at Terrace Spring, Tyson. There's a boardwalk. It'll be easy to walk around with the baby. Dax, you've never touched a tree before. Let's get out and find a branch.

Found one! Give me your hand, Dax. Grab on! Do you feel the flaky bark on the tree? Don't touch any pine needles; they're sharp!

Wow, Dax—the first rock you ever touched was at the Grand Canyon, and the first tree you ever touched was at the oldest national park in the world. That's incredible!

Sightseeing and exploring has been so much fun, but there's no place like home. Ozzie, are you ready to get back to your own bed and to your spot on the couch? I know Dax is looking forward to relaxing at home.

What an adventure. We made so many wonderful, everlasting memories together.

The Meaning of the Name Dax:

(DAKS) 1. Origin: a masculine personal name borrowed from a medieval English surname deriving from a nickname, from the Old Germanic *dachs* "badger," traced to the Proto-Germanic root *thahsuz* "badger," quite literally, "builder, the animal that builds," in reference to how the badger occupies his time; 2. Historic: the badger was sacred to the ancient Indo-European tribal people who admired the animal for his fighting spirit and survival skills, symbolic of their own tenacity, courage and sheer strength of will; such a surname would have evolved from a byname given to a fellow exhibiting traits of feisty persistence and enthusiasm (one "full of life"); the surname is first found in Germany ("Dach") in the early 13th century and in East Anglia, England ("Dacke") by the late 13th century; 3. Usage: its use as a masculine first name is found regularly only since the early 21st century, inspired by the fashionable surname-naming trend and also propelled by the popularity of similar sounding one-syllable colloquial names like Max, Jax, and Pax. Personality traits include: powerful, inspirational, ambitious, bright, highly intuitive, uplifting, charismatic, independent, and creative.

Source: Name Stories®

I hope **Dax's Big Adventure!** inspires you to get out and experience the beauty our world has to offer: the warm sunshine, the cool breeze, and the bright blue sky. It amazes me to see what nature does; Dax seems to be more alert after spending so much time in the open air. Take the time to slow down to be present in the moment; soak it all in, every second of it–that's how life should be lived. As we've made many memories with Dax, we've learned that the simplest moments mean the most to us. There's joy in each day, even if you have to search a little harder to find it. We spend many of our days searching for those little sparks of joy.

When life throws you curveballs, make every effort to stay positive. It may not come easy, but try to focus on what to be grateful for. Having a healthy mindset and living with a perspective of gratitude can be essential when going through difficult times.

One of Dax's doctors told us that Dax has enough of his brainstem to feel emotion; he can feel love. That's all we really need in life, right? I ask that whenever you see a dragonfly, think of Dax. The neurological findings in his MRI show a "dragonfly-like" cerebellum. Much like Dax, dragonflies symbolize self-realization, understanding the deeper meaning of life, taking the time to reconnect with our own strength and happiness, overcoming times of hardship, and living life to the fullest.

To read more about Dax, visit our blog!
www.thestoryofdaxwilder.com

CPSIA information can be obtained
at www.ICGtesting.com
Printed in the USA
LVHW070318120523
746758LV00003B/73

9 780228 864080